The FIREPLACE Book

an idea book of fireplace designs

by the editors of Aberdeen's Magazine of Masonry Construction

Editor: Kari Moosmann
Art Director: John Baggio

 The Aberdeen Group

426 South Westgate, Addison, Illinois 60101
Telephone: 708-543-0870 Fax: 708.543.3112

The
FIREPLACE
Book

an idea book of fireplace designs

published by
The Aberdeen Group
426 South Westgate
Addison, IL 60101

10 9 8 7 6 5 4 3 2

ISBN 0-924659-49-1

Item No. 4510

CONTENTS

WELCOME TO

The FIREPLACE Book

Building or remodeling your home is an exciting experience, but it can present you with an intimidating array of choices. Few of those choices can affect the value, comfort, and enjoyment of your home as strongly as the fireplace.

We've published this book to make choosing masonry fireplaces a little less daunting, and to give you some idea of their nearly limitless possibilities. The photographs, many of which originally appeared in *Aberdeen's Magazine of Masonry Construction*, will help you, your architect, your builder, and your masonry contractor come up with a fireplace design that exactly suits your home and your lifestyle.

Why choose masonry?

An all-masonry fireplace, properly constructed with a firebrick firebox, a clay flue liner, and a face and chimney of brick, concrete block, or stone, is the traditional first choice for many reasons. Masonry is the most durable material you can use. It adds the most to a home's resale value and, in some areas, reduces insurance rates. And it offers the greatest variety of sizes, shapes, colors, and textures to help you make a unique architectural statement.

Factors to consider

When planning your fireplace, consider all of these points:

- **Size.** How large are the room and the wall where the fireplace will be located? Your fireplace should be large enough to serve as a focal point, but not so big that it overwhelms the space. Firebox size also is important. Too large a fire can make a small room uncomfortably warm. Too small a fire may not create the atmosphere you want.
- **Heat.** How much will you rely on the fireplace to heat the space? If you want the fireplace to be a supplemental heat source, incorporate an air circulation system into the design or consider a masonry heater (see page 47). These units take full advantage of masonry's ability to store and radiate heat.
- **Convenience.** How much time and effort will you spend in starting and maintaining a fire? Consider including a gas starter or even a gas log for the greatest ease of operation. Include an ash pit to make cleaning the fireplace neater and easier. Decide whether your fireplace design should include a storage bin for firewood.
- **Style.** The fireplaces in this book only suggest the range of possibilities. From comfortably rustic to dignified traditional to sleekly contemporary, masonry's variety makes it suitable for any style of architecture and interior design. The range of colors, textures, patterns, and scales offered by brick, concrete block, and natural stone is virtually infinite.
- **Safe, efficient operation.** You'll want your fireplace to burn brightly, to draw smoke efficiently up and out the chimney, and to minimize any risk of a house or chimney fire. Make sure the design you choose provides for outside air to feed combustion. This is especially important in today's tightly sealed, energy-efficient homes. And make sure the design and construction follow all applicable building and fire code requirements.

A custom-built masonry fireplace can satisfy all these needs and desires. We hope you'll be informed and inspired by the photographs and articles in this book. We expect you'll enjoy your new fireplace for years to come.

Ken Hooker

Ken Hooker
Editor
Magazine of Masonry Construction

CONVENTIONAL
Fireplaces

Conventional masonry fireplaces add warmth and life to family rooms, restaurants, and even bank lobbies. Their styles can vary dramatically—with brick, stone, or concrete masonry used in contemporary, rustic, country, and traditional designs. These fireplaces are called conventional because they share a standard inner fireplace design (see page 61).

Though this section shows only a sampling of what is possible, you will get an idea of the range of materials and styles that can be mixed and matched.

Peggy Johnson, Ashe Brick

Ron Ericksen

Frank Rourke

Top, Left This arch is created by corbeling three courses of rowlock brick. The same effect is used to finish the firebox and sides of the profile. This design is also used on the outside of the house, over the windows. The Ashe Molded Williamsburg brick is used in a basketweave pattern to produce the transitional appearance.

Top, Right Common brick and black-colored mortar accent the traditional-style fireplace. The raised hearth and wood mantel shelf provide a warm feeling.

Bottom A brick segmental arch, laid in two rowlock courses, gives this fireplace a traditional look. The firebox area is recessed one brick width, providing a dimensional accent. Masonry contractor: Frank Rourke, Waltham, MA.

Opposite page A variety of arched openings are found in this fireplace wall. Logs, vases, and other nicknacks are found inhabiting many of the openings in the wall. General Shale's Centennial brick provide the faded brick look of an early American design.

The Brick Institute of America

The Brick Institute of America

The Brick Institute of America

Watkins Concrete Block Co.

Ed Glass Masonry

Opposite page, Top A traditional segmental arch laid in a soldier course.

Opposite page, Bottom, Left A country-looking semicircular arch.

Opposite page, Bottom, Right A semicircular arch frames the opening of this fireplace. In this contemporary design the top of the firebox opening is rounded, but the sides are straight. Masonry contractor: Alan Reeves, All Star Masonry, Albuquerque, NM.

Top, Left Arch upon arch upon arch is the design repeated around the firebox and on the wall above. Chocolate-colored mortar blends with Glen-Gery's Rawhide 840 brick. A contemporary approach to using arches. Masonry contractor: Mike Wees, Omaha, NE.

Top, Right A soldier course arch and a basketweave-bond pattern highlight this early American fireplace. Glen-Gery's handmade brick give this style an authentic look. The heat exchanger in the grate and the ceiling fan help spread the warmth throughout the first floor of the home. Masonry contractor: Ed Glass Masonry, Erie, PA.

Bottom, Right A wooden mantel shelf dissects the arched recessed area around and above the firebox. What starts out as a traditional design is transformed into a contemporary style. Masonry contractor: Chimney Works Inc., Williamsport, PA.

General Shale Products Corp.

Lori Ashley

Sandi Johnson

Top, Left This home is dominated by brick. General Shale's Colonial Bardstown brick are used for the fireplace, the outside of the house, the driveway, and for a series of low walls and planters in the front yard. The traditional elements are strong, yet simple, modernizing the traditional appearance. Designer: David Sullivan. Masonry contractor: Bob Conway.

Bottom, Left Not all fireplace walls are as multipurpose as this one is. Besides a fireplace and a wood box, the brick wall contains a refrigerated 40-bottle wine cooler, an oak wine and glass rack, and a brick counter with a mirror behind it. The used brick provide some variety in the color and texture of this contemporary fireplace wall. Masonry contractor: Greg Johnson, Brick Crafters Masonry, Mission Viejo, CA.

Top, Right Black mortar accents the rustic brick used in this country room. The large basketweave-bond panel is centered over the yellow pine mantel shelf. Circulating air vents move the air, warmed by the fire into the room. Masonry contractor: Charles Ashley Construction Inc., Swansea, MA.

Opposite page The brick in this fireplace look old but they're not. They are Old English genuine handmade brick from the Old Carolina Brick Co. The appearance of yesterday's brickwork adds a soft edge to a normally sharp-edged, traditional fireplace.

Top An elegant, rich ambiance is created by the dark colors of the brick, from Acme Brick Co., in this traditional fireplace. The vertical lines complement the inset herringbone pattern and the wood mantel shelf above the soldier course at the firebox opening. A raised brick hearth brings the firebox to eye level with the adjacent furnishings.

Opposite page, Top This typical masonry fireplace takes a contemporary twist with an extended hearth that serves as a window seat. An all-brick mantel shelf and arched firebox opening add flair to the Kings Mountain white wire cut brick. Architects: David Campbell and Susie Allen. Masonry contractor: David Nelson Masonry, Naples, FL.

Opposite page, Bottom, Left Brick detailing surrounds this traditional-looking fireplace wall. From the columns framing the wall and forming a squared-off arch on the top, to the "M" above the mantel shelf, the detailing gives the fireplace wall a self-contained, finished look. Masonry contractor: Larry Hanner Masonry Construction, Bloomfield, MO.

Opposite page, Bottom Right "Modified traditional" describes this fireplace. The traditional wood mantel shelf is missing from this design and log storage is built in. Four bond patterns are used to accent the unraised hearth, fireplace face, sides, and the top and bottom of the firebox and log storage area.

Scott Shook

Bon Tool Co.

Carolyn Cole

Duffy Stowers for General Shale Products Corp.

J. Andrew Weber Photography

Opposite page, Top An American Southwest flavor pervades this 16x6x20-foot masonry dividing structure between a great room and kitchen area. The wall is multileveled and includes an air-circulating fireplace with an angled hearth, entertainment niches, alcoves, and masonry shelves. There are brick arches on the kitchen side. Robinson's Greymoor brick was used. Designers: Vern Swisher, Pam Swisher, Swisher Builders, Toledo, OH. Masonry contractor: Dake Masonry, Toledo, OH.

Opposite page, Bottom The wooden mantel shelf, rectangular fireplace opening with a raised hearth, and the overall crisp, clean appearance is reminiscent of a traditional fireplace. But the brickwork is unique, scaling down the width a half a brick at a time, from the mantel shelf to the chimney. The contemporary design uses General Shale's Jefferson Wade Tudor brick. Architect: Theil & Associates. Masonry contractor: Oxford Development Co.

Top The masonry in this fireplace, with its conventional running bond pattern, is clean and simple...an appropriately business-like tone for a bank lobby. The uncomplicated lines of the brick (with brownish mortar) provide a good backdrop for the dramatic hood, which was handcrafted in copper and brass by a European-trained master blacksmith.

Bon Tool Co.

Scott Shook

Glen-Gery Corp.

Top, Left This circular free-standing fireplace has a raised hearth. A header stack bond pattern is used to carry through the contemporary look. The design incorporates built-in log storage.

Top, Right A curved mantle, hearth, and face complete the circular design of this fireplace. Nestled in a corner between a door and a window, the Bickerstaff wood-molded half brick gives a rough edge to the contemporary design. Masonry contractor: David Nelson Masonry, Naples, FL.

Bottom This postmodern, cylindrical, three-dimensional effect fireplace was designed for the architect's own family room. Glen-Gery's shasta brown extruded brick provides the warm tone. Architect: Pierce Architecture, Bailey's Crossroads, VA. Masonry contractor: Gruver & Cooley, Washington, DC.

Opposite page A contemporary inside-corner design fits into the family room with minimal disruption of wall space. This curved fireplace with a raised hearth was added 10 years after the house was built. The brick matches that used on the exterior of the home. Masonry contractor: Jorgen Bohansen, Palatine, IL.

J. Andrew Weber Photography

© Wheeler Photographics

Gerald R. White

Opposite page This dramatic, contemporary fireplace wall is a total energy storage system, storing sunlight and heat from the fireplace which is then circulated throughout the room by interior flues. Architect: Edmund Stevens Associates Inc., Lincoln, MA.

Top, Left Waterstruck brick are continuously corbeled on this two-story, four-sided fireplace. This modern design decorates the inside of an East Coast restaurant. Architect: Edmund Stevens Associates Inc., Lincoln, MA.

Top, Right The Gloucester brick's speckled coloring accents this contemporary two-sided see-through fireplace. Designer: Gerald R. White. Masonry contractor: Gerald R. White.

Top Heat radiates from all four sides of this corbeled brick fireplace. The common sand-struck brick used are almost secondary to the contemporary design. In addition to warming the tile-floored living and dining rooms, the fireplace creates an eye-catching division between the two rooms. Architect: Edmund Stevens Associates Inc., Lincoln, MA.

Opposite page This high, shallow, elliptically arched fireplace is a contemporary expression of a rustic design. White mortar accents the salmon-colored special bullnose brick. The fireplace transforms from a square-cornered base to an arched fireplace body to a four-lobed main chimney with bullnose corners. A soapstone woodburning bake oven is on the backside of the fireplace. Designer: Louis P. Salamone, Norfolk, CT. Masonry contractor: Ed Cichon, Seal Masonry, Winsted, CT.

Judy Mead

© Ronni Nienstedt

Top Mason Don C. Voorhees designed and built this fireplace in the master bedroom of his home. Because the firebox is elevated, the viewer has the pleasure of looking directly at the fire from the bed. The fireplace is also the focal point of the room. Although it is an unusual design, it is traditional in the elements it uses—wood mantel shelf and pillars framing the fireplace and a square firebox opening. In this design the slightly raised hearth is made of the same brick used on the fireplace. Designer and masonry contractor: Don C. Voorhees, Pattenburg, NJ.

Christopher Herbert

Jerry W. Brailsford

Christopher Herbert

Top, Left "Nectar Delight" is the title of this contemporary work. A simple fireplace design is used that doesn't compete with the sculpture. The sculpture, framed on both sides by vertical columns of projecting brick, is sculpted out of Interstate Brick's warm-toned Baja Brown brick. Masonry contractor and sculptor: Brailsford Inc., Springville, UT.

Bottom, Left Deer frolic across this modern sculptured brick fireplace wall. To produce this masterpiece, Interstate Brick's Canyon Rose brick were carved while still green. Then, the sculpture was dismantled and each brick was numbered and sent to the brick producer for drying and finishing. The brick were then laid in the proper order. Masonry contractor and sculptor: Brailsford Inc., Springville, UT.

Top, Right Masons seem to build this fireplace before your eyes. Many elements of the "Nectar Delight" fireplace are found in this one as well: a simple contemporary design, vertical columns projecting on both sides of the fireplace, and a raised hearth. A hand-carved mantel shelf and a brick accent around the fireplace opening vary the design. Masonry contractor and sculptor: Brailsford Inc., Springville, UT.

Jay Tschetter

© John Spofforth

© Kris K. King

Opposite page, Top, Left A tree-of-life mural was carved into Delta Brick's 8x8x4-inch brick used in this contemporary fireplace. Built-in air intakes, heating chambers, and fans circulate the heated air to the living room. The chimney splits, allowing a small Juliet balcony to project. Sculptor: Paula Collins, Denton, TX. Contractor: Dan Miller Construction Co., Starkville, MS.

Opposite page, Top, Right Buffalo roam free in this carefully centered mural. Decorative square brick provide accents along the sides of this traditional design, framing the mural and the firebox. Glen-Gery's brick was used. Sculptor: Jay Tschetter, Lincoln, NE.

Opposite page, Bottom "The Weiner Walls" was commissioned for a private residence in Athens, OH. The expressive modern fireplace wall, measuring 7½x46 feet, was both designed and built by the sculptor, an experienced bricklayer with an M.F.A. in Painting and Sculpture. Masonry contractor and sculptor: John Spofforth, Athens, OH.

Top Knowledge and learning are depicted on two back-to-back contemporary fireplaces in a university center. The fireplace area, a central gathering place, also houses the elevator. The murals, "Knowledge I" and "Knowledge II," are carved of Acme Brick's Perla Grey brick. Architect: H.T.B. Architects Inc., Tulsa, OK. Sculptor: Mara Smith, Architectural Murals in Brick, Seattle, WA. Masonry contractor: Brazeal Masonry Contractor, Tulsa, OK.

Bottom, Right Carved brick swans are centered above an oak mantel shelf in this traditional design. The decorative brick face includes a tall arch containing a herringbone pattern. Architect: Larry O. Thorondsen, Bothell, WA. Sculptor: Mara Smith, Architectural Murals in Brick, Seattle, WA. Masonry contractor: Hallock's Masonry Inc., Issaquah, WA.

© Kris K. King

Concrete Masonry Fireplaces

Top Split-faced concrete brick provides a brilliant white look for this fireplace. The contemporary design is highlighted by a raised hearth. Architect: William G. Phillips, AIA, Midland, MI. Masonry contractor: Larry Lovely Masonry, Midland, MI.

Bottom The offset split face of these concrete block give this freestanding fireplace a rugged beauty. The block manufacturer created the surface texture and pattern by splitting one large block on two parallel planes, creating four different split surfaces. This contemporary fireplace is found in a restaurant. The same material was used for the exterior walls of the restaurant.

Opposite page This floor-to-ceiling fireplace is faced with 2-, 4-, and 6-inch-high concrete masonry laid in a coursed ashlar pattern. Black mortar joints provide a striking contrast to the light gray split-face block. Masonry contractor: Spetla Brothers Masonry, Middlegrove, NY.

22

James N. Boorn Photography

Paul Beswick. Used with permission of Jimco Stone Centers, Tampa, FL.

Top This contemporary fireplace is done in coursed ashlar using quartzite stone. The same stone has been incorporated into the raised hearth and the mantel. Simple, clean lines give this fireplace a touch of formality, and variations in the stone add interest to the design.

Opposite page, Top This solid masonry mass absorbs and stores heat and, by convection, circulates the heated air throughout the house. The red sandstone, Cassel Rock from Luck Stone Co., is accented with a red mortar. Designer: M. Scott Watkins, Arlington, VA. General contractor: Watkins Contracting Inc., Arlington, VA.

Opposite page, Bottom, Left A sunburst explodes over the mantel shelf of this fireplace. The contemporary design is heat-circulating and uses Maryland Ledge Rock stone for the fireplace, ash wood for the sunburst and mantel shelf and Maryland Patio stone for the hearth. Masonry contractor: John Stefanko, Elizabeth, PA.

Opposite page, Bottom, Right From floor to ceiling, this wall is covered with cast stone. A simple rectangular fireplace opening and a log storage area interrupt the massive stone wall. A green mantel shelf extends over both the firebox and the log storage area. Wisconsin Weather-Edge stone creates this contemporary design.

Jerry Mesmer, Adam's Studio

John Stefanko

Robert Buhl for Stucco Stone Products Inc.

Georgia Marble Co.

Top A fireplace wall always makes a bold statement, especially when done in large stones such as these Alabama marble chunks. The large expanse of the contemporary wall is made more interesting by the various shades of brown and beige and by the shadows cast by the edges of the stone. Here it is best to leave the dramatic sweep of the wall uninterrupted by a mantel shelf.

Bottom Huge chunks of white Montana travertine are used for this rustic rubble stone fireplace. The flush hearth is made of black Vermont slate. Masonry contractor: J. E. Frisch, Lopez Quarries Masonry Heaters/Firecrest Fireplace Corp., Everett, WA.

Opposite page The colorful quartzite veneer matches the stone used on the home's exterior. Notice the raised hearth and mantel shelf are wider than the mantel—features easily incorporated into contemporary inside-corner designs.

J. E. Frisch

Georgia Marble Co.

Georgia Marble Co.

Ronald Urness Residence

Georgia Marble Co.

Opposite page This raised-hearth contemporary fireplace stretches from the floor to the exposed beam of a cathedral ceiling. The cream-colored Alabama marble chunks and the white mortar provide a striking contrast to the dark, paneled walls, while the smooth wooden mantel shelf enhances the texture of the stone.

Top, Left A built-in conversation pit faces the hand-split stone fireplace of soft rose and cream tones. Coral mountain stone from New Mexico creates the contemporary Southwestern-style fireplace wall with a built-in wood box. Designer: William Lyttle, New Brighton, MN. Masonry contractor: Eddy Quam Masonry Construction, Ramsey, MN.

Bottom, Left A brick hearth, arch, and mantel shelf pillars accent the stonework in this rustic design. Masonry contractor: Thompson Masonry, Wooster, OH.

Top, Right These aren't chunks of snow; they're pieces of white Georgia marble. Light-colored stone and mortar, when teamed up with a full-height fireplace in a room full of darker colors, can become a dramatic, contemporary focal point. A mantel shelf in a warm brown keeps the bright stone from being too overpowering.

Ron Erickson

Top This traditional fireplace topped with a mantel shelf is constructed of rough-dressed ashlar. The same stone is used for the hearth. As with most ashlar structures, the crisp lines impart a cool, formal look.

Opposite page, Top, Left Natural Florida-cut coral was laid in a random ashlar pattern to construct this fireplace. The raised hearth and wooden mantel shelf are part of the traditional design. Designer: David Nelson Masonry, Naples, FL. Masonry contractor: David Nelson Masonry, Naples, FL.

Opposite page, Bottom The hand-chiseled stone found in medieval European buildings spurred the creation of this Classic Castle stone. The focal point of this contemporary concrete fireplace is the contrasting lintel of precast concrete; precast concrete also is incorporated into the raised hearth. The rough stone and smooth concrete make for an interesting juxtaposition of color and texture.

Opposite page, Right Hand-dressed dimensioned granite is a traditional material, but here it is used in a contemporary design. The first floor of this design has one alcove for a woodstove and one for wood storage. The second floor fireplace has a roman arch with a dropped keystone. The hearth is slate. Designer: David Johnstone Masonry & Design, Errington, BC, Canada. Masonry contractor: David Johnstone Masonry & Design, Errington, BC, Canada.

Scott Shook

Rusty Joerin, Woodsgift Photography

Stucco Stone Products Inc.

Thermal Energy Storage Systems Inc.

Lori Ashley

J. E. Frisch

Opposite page In the days of old, the streets of San Francisco were paved with cobblestones that had been used as ballasts in the ships from Europe. This warm, rustic fireplace re-creates the look of cobblestone. Massive wood beams frame the top of this fireplace wall, giving the room a cozy feeling. The raised hearth is made from the same cobblestone-effect cast stone.

Top, Left The off-center design of this raised-hearth fireplace lends a relaxed, rustic feeling to the room. The shale chunks fit together tightly, making mortar joints barely discernible. A wedge-shaped stone over the arched opening mimics a keystone. At the wall's edges, stones are alternately laid vertically and horizontally. The same dark shale is used for the hearth and mantel shelf. Masonry contractor: Luigi D'Alto, Redding, CT.

Top, Right Here the firebox is set back and a 35° angled hood extends over the opening. A bluestone raised hearth matches the design of the hood. Architect: A. Rousseau Construction Inc., Swansea, MA. Masonry contractor: Charles Ashley Construction Inc., Swansea, MA.

Bottom, Right Ten feet wide and from floor to ceiling, this fireplace is framed on all sides with wood. Montana flagstone is used to provide a finished, contemporary look. Built-in log storage is an additional feature. Architect: Don McKee, Anacortes, WA. Masonry contractor: J. E. Frisch, Lopez Quarries Masonry Heaters/Firecrest Fireplace Corp., Everett, WA.

J. E. Frisch

Wallace Reeves

J. E. Frisch

Thermal Energy Storage Systems Inc.

Opposite page, Top, Left Fieldstone is carefully laid to form an arch above the firebox. The early American design features a matching raised hearth. The fireplace is reinforced to support floor and roof beams. Architect: Howard Peterson, Lopez, WA. Masonry contractor: J. E. Frisch, Lopez Quarries Masonry Heaters/Firecrest Fireplace Corp., Everett, WA.

Opposite page, Top, Right Random, rough marble chunks, varying from 6 to 18 inches, create this rustic, heat-circulating fireplace. The Pecan Chunk marble is framed by wooden beams that extend to meet the ceiling beams. Architect: Jack Wade, Wade Block and Tile Co. Inc., Gautier, MS. Masonry contractor: Dale Mathison, Ocean Springs, MS.

Opposite page, Bottom A wood storage area with a display shelf is featured in this rustic design. Bedrock is used for the face of the fireplace. Architect: Howard Peterson, Lopez, WA. Masonry contractor: J. E. Frisch, Lopez Quarries Masonry Heaters/Firecrest Fireplace Corp., Everett, WA.

Top An arched opening and wall of rough-dressed stone create a fireplace reminiscent of pioneer days. Careful planning is required to fit the stones together and keep mortar joints uniform. Protruding stones support the wooden mantel shelf. Masonry contractor: Gary Hoffman, Califon, NJ.

Philip Wegener Kantor

Stucco Stone Products Inc.

Top, Left This solid stone rustic fireplace produces up to 60,000 Btus/hour with its heat-circulating system. The hearth and mantel shelf are made of flagstone. The granite stone used for the fireplace matches that used on the exterior of the house and on a retaining wall in the yard. Architect: Doug Walter, Denver, CO. Masonry contractor: Dave Lee Masonry, Arvada, CO.

Top, Right Dark-colored mortar accents the curved edges of the cast stone used for this rustic fireplace. Modeled after the smooth, rounded rocks found in streams and riverbeds, the Earth Blend River Rock is carefully fitted together like pieces of a jigsaw puzzle. The nearly-square hearth stones also are cast of concrete. Masonry contractor: R. D. Heath, Stonecraft Masonry, Napa, CA.

Opposite page, Top, Left A cubbyhole for storing wood and a decorative recess on the right side are two features of this contemporary cast stone fireplace wall. The concrete stone—Lake Tahoe Blend River Rock—covers the wall up to the cathedral ceiling. A raised hearth of gray concrete matches the color of the mortar used to lay the stone.

Opposite page, Bottom, Left This cast stone fieldstone replicates the natural stone native to the Michigan area. Michigan Fieldstone is used to create this simple, traditional design. A hooded effect is created by projecting the center area of stone above the fireplace opening.

Opposite page, Top, Right The uncut fieldstone used was chosen for the shape, color, and texture of each stone. The Michigan glacial stone gives the viewer of this rustic fireplace a perception of movement. Masonry contractor: Tripp Stone Co., Hastings, MI.

Opposite page, Bottom, Right Large and small pieces of light green Watuga stone were laid to form an almost cave-like entrance shape for this contemporary fireplace. The rosewood mantel was cut to fit the fireplace's profile. Designer: Everett Hess, Chesapeake, VA. Masonry contractor: Danny Hill, Snow Jr. & King, Norfolk, VA.

Stucco Stone Products Inc.

Thomas Chandler, Visual Artistry

Everett and Anita Hess Residence. Photo by Everett Hess.

Stucco Stone Products Inc.

J. E. Frisch

J. E. Frisch

J. E. Frisch

The Photographers & Co.

Opposite page, Top, Left The raised hearth and built-in cantilevered mantel shelf match the bedrock face stone of the fireplace. This massive rustic design is also heat circulating. Architect: Dallas Olsen, Everett, WA. Masonry contractor: J. E. Frisch, Lopez Quarries Masonry Heaters/Firecrest Fireplace Corp., Everett, WA.

Opposite page, Top, Right This modern rustic design is a two-sided corner fireplace. Columbia River Basalt stone provides a rugged feeling. Architect: Robert Butterfield, Everett, WA. Masonry contractor: J. E. Frisch, Lopez Quarries Masonry Heaters/Firecrest Fireplace Corp., Everett, WA.

Opposite page, Bottom Beach rock is fitted closely in this rustic design. The raised hearth matches the fireplace face. The large firebox opening, 40 inches, is reminiscent of the pioneer days. Masonry contractor: J. E. Frisch, Lopez Quarries Masonry Heaters/Firecrest Fireplace Corp., Everett, WA.

Top This fireplace begins on the first floor in a room with 7-foot ceilings. It extends up to the third floor with an arch that is angled to match the ceiling of the living room. Alcove Bluestone, from Adam Ross Cut Stone Co. Inc., was used for this massive heat-circulating fireplace. Architect: Raymond R. Lammon Architects, Troy, NY. Masonry contractor: Bruce O'Brien, Alcove, NY.

RUMFORD
Fireplaces

Rumford fireplaces, commonly built between 1796 and 1850, are now seeing a resurgence in popularity. The different shape and proportions of the Rumford firebox (see page 60) make it a more efficient heat source than a conventional fireplace. Thomas Jefferson was so impressed by the design's efficiency that he had Rumford fireplaces built in Monticello.

The Rumford design can be adapted to almost any fireplace style or material. The examples shown in this section are typical designs.

Lew Coopey

Top An early American cooking fireplace, complete with a bread oven and log storage, is an authentic replication of a 1798 fireplace. This fireplace is found in a replicated 1798 New England Saltbox house built in Phoenix, AZ. Designer and masonry contractor: Jim Buckley, Buckley Rumford Fireplace Co., Columbus, OH.

Opposite page, Top This is the most traditional style of Rumford fireplace. Found in the same house as the fireplace above, but in a different room, it also is an authentic reproduction of a 1798 Rumford fireplace. Designer and masonry contractor: Jim Buckley, Buckley Rumford Fireplace Co., Columbus, OH.

Opposite page, Bottom, Left Marble surrounds the opening of this traditional Rumford fireplace. The sharp details on the wooden mantel shelf give a formal air to the room. Designer: Randy Mason, Marietta, OH. Masonry contractor: Paul King, Marietta, OH.

Opposite page, Bottom, Right An 1876 Victorian coal-burning fireplace was converted to a wood-burning Rumford fireplace, retaining the original 20x27x12-inch opening. The original marbleized slate mantel was reset. Designer and masonry contractor: Jim Buckley, Buckley Rumford Fireplace Co., Columbus, OH.

Lew Coopey

R. K. Rega

Emery Photography

Susan Milazzo

J. E. Frisch

J. E. Frisch

Opposite page, Top, Left In the winter, the full moon shines through the window in the chimney of this fireplace. The contemporary Rumford fireplace features brick detailing around the window and on the borders of the fireplace. The hearth is made of inlaid marble. Masonry contractor: Etter Mason Contractors, Howell, NJ.

Opposite page, Top, Right The half circle hood over a Rumford-style firebox allows for a 180° view of the fire. The hearth and face stone are a Montana native flagstone. Masonry contractor: J. E. Frisch, Lopez Quarries/Firecrest Fireplace Corp., Everett, WA.

Opposite page, Bottom The double arch around this Rumford firebox opening makes the opening appear larger than it actually is. An opal stone fireplace, Italian marble cantilevered hearth, and an Idaho Mica slate lower hearth create a polished, yet rustic look. Masonry contractor: J. E. Frisch, Lopez Quarries/Firecrest Fireplace Corp., Everett, WA.

Top The arched opening of this fireplace is framed by the wooden mantel shelf and timber framing around it. A soldier course at the top adds interest to the rustic design. The fireplace has a five-sided, modified Rumford fire chamber.

MASONRY HEATERS

Masonry heaters and stoves are an efficient, ecologically responsible way to heat homes. Long popular in Europe, masonry heaters are attracting new interest in America. A masonry heater uses less wood than a conventional fireplace or woodstove, heats longer and more evenly, and releases less pollution (see page 63).

These benefits are provided by heaters in a wide variety of styles. Some resemble conventional fireplaces. Some, such as Finnish soapstone heaters and Swedish or German tile stoves, derive from European traditions. Others, are custom designed for specific rooms. The examples shown here suggest the distinctiveness and diversity of masonry heaters.

Biofire Inc.

Biofire Inc.

Top, Left A European-styled masonry heater is faced with decorative refractory tiles. This type of heater is also called a tile stove. Masonry contractor: Heinz Flurer, Biofire Inc., Salt Lake City, UT.

Top, Right This heater is contemporary with its circular shape and rounded tile. The white ceramic tiles are applied over the concrete masonry firebox, heat channels, and chimney. Designer: Royal Crown European Fireplaces Inc., Rockford, IL.

Bottom, Right The tile on this European-styled heater is warm, not hot, to touch, making the wooden bench a safe and warm place to sit. Masonry contractor: Heinz Flurer, Biofire Inc., Salt Lake City, UT.

Opposite page A traditional style in an untraditional material...stucco. The stucco finish acts as a sponge, absorbing the heat of the fire and slowly releasing it into the room. Designer: Royal Crown European Fireplaces Inc., Rockford, IL.

Biofire Inc.

Top This contemporary soapstone heater has a convection system to help circulate the warm air throughout the home. The Finnish design is often called a thermal mass fireplace. Designer: Tulikivi Group North America, North Lebanon, NH.

Bottom, Left Serpentine arch stones are found around the door of this soapstone heater. The traditional design produces heat for 24 hours after burning a vigorous fire for 2 to 3 hours. Designer: Tulikivi Group North America, North Lebanon, NH.

Opposite page, Top Decorative tile accents the stucco finish. A tile bench surrounds the European-styled heater, providing a warm place to sit. Masonry contractor: Heinz Flurer, Biofire Inc., Salt Lake City, UT.

Opposite page, Bottom, Left Stucco gives a smooth, contemporary look to a multilevel masonry heater. The different levels provide extra shelf space for displays. Masonry contractor: Heinz Flurer, Biofire Inc., Salt Lake City, UT.

Opposite page, Bottom, Right The European-styled masonry heater has a stucco finish over an interior of refractory brick. Masonry contractor: Heinz Flurer, Biofire Inc., Salt Lake City, UT.

Biofire Inc.

Biofire Inc.

Biofire Inc.

Phil Bell

J. E. Frisch

Bavarian Stoves & Masonry Inc.

Erik Nilsen

J. E. Frisch

Erik Nilsen

Opposite page, Top Granite river rock and used brick make up this rustic design. This Finnish contra-flow fireplace also has a brick bake oven and a cook top. Architect: Larry Raffety, Livingston, MT. Masonry contractor: Ron Pihl, Cornerstone Masonry, Pray, MT.

Opposite page, Bottom, Left Here a Swedish-style masonry heater is built of River Rock cobblestones. The wood storage area has a display shelf above it. Hot water coil and preheat tank were also built in. Architect: Craig Knoll, Monroe, WA. Masonry contractor: J. E. Frisch, Lopez Quarries/Firecrest Fireplace Corp., Everett, WA.

Opposite page, Bottom, Right A Kachelofen is another type of masonry heater or masonry heat storage system. This design was developed in Germany. Designer and masonry contractor: Bavarian Stoves & Masonry Inc., Seward, PA.

Top, Left Brick is accented with a soapstone mantel shelf and soapstone keystones in arches on the front of this masonry heater. The hearth is made of blue stone. A large log storage area was built into the traditional design. Architect: Jeff Wenger, Jackson, NH. Masonry contractor: Thermal Mass Inc., Dalton, NH.

Bottom, Left Used brick gives this thermal storage fireplace an old, traditional appearance. Blue stone was used for the mantel shelf and side shelf. Masonry contractor: Thermal Mass Inc., Dalton, NH.

Top, Right Chamfered corners provide a special effect in this contemporary Swedish heater. The brick face extends to create a wood storage box and a VCR-TV ledge. Carrib brick from Mutual Materials are used for the face and slate from Lopez Quarries for the hearth. Masonry contractor: J. E. Frisch, Lopez Quarries/Firecrest Fireplace Corp., Everett, WA.

CHIMNEYS

Masonry chimneys are more than a functional feature on a house. Chimneys are now decorative showpieces, especially on large custom homes. Corbeling, distinctive bond patterns, double flues, and insets are only some of the techniques a mason can use to create a special design for your home.

Top, Left Square brick columns, built at a 45° angle to the chimney face, encase the flues of this chimney. At the bottom of the columns, soldier courses are used for a wash. Soldier and rowlock courses also are used at the top of the chimney.

Top, Right Large chunky stones create this rustic chimney. The bottom half of the chimney expands into a stone wall made of the same material.

Center, Left A richly textured chimney is the result of dogtoothed insets, bullnose stretchers, corbels, soldier courses, and panels in herringbone bond. The most eye-catching feature is the chimney's three spiral columns topped with decorative clay chimney pots.

Center, Right Corbeled brick near the top of this chimney and vertical bands of protruding headers with corbeled bottoms create heavy shadow lines. The bottom of each vertical band stops a few courses below the bottom of the band before it.

Bottom, Right The chimney of this home has two recessed basketweave panels and a wash of soldier courses. Single and double soldier courses also are used at the top of the chimney.

Opposite page, Top, Left A semicircular arch graces the top of this two-flued chimney. Corbeled brick are around the chimney top. A narrow opening in the body of the chimney reveals the sky.

Opposite page, Top, Right Square stones are carefully laid together, almost hiding the mortar on this chimney. Three courses of stone are cantilevered out to the finished stack.

Opposite page, Center, Left An arrow-shaped inset on this chimney draws the eye up to the corbeling at the top of the chimney.

Opposite page, Center, Right Relatively simple in design, this chimney is accented by a deeply corbeled top and a white diamond-shaped stone.

Opposite page, Bottom, Left The double-flue chimney of this residence has a center recessed panel of brick in herringbone bond. Vertical header courses of lighter brick frame the recessed panel.

Opposite page, Bottom, Right To make the basketweave pattern in the center of this chimney more discernible, white mortar was used with the reddish-brown brick. The basketweave panel is framed by headers and topped with an arch.

John Stefanko

Jack Della Bitta for Stonesmith

Britt Stokes, Acme Brick Co.

General Shale

Britt Stokes, Acme Brick Co.

Britt Stokes, Acme Brick Co.

Judy Nead for Seal Masonry

Robinson Brick Co.

Scott Shook for David Nelson Masonry

General Shale

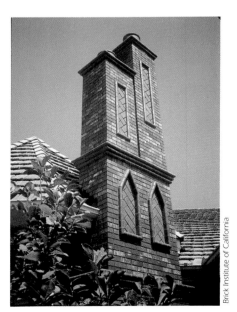

Brick Institute of California

Top, Left Recessed corners on this chimney lead the eye up to the slightly larger chimney opening. Unique clay chimney pots are the focal point of the structure.

Top, Right Headers in a modified garden wall bond embellish the top and arched center panel of this chimney.

Bottom, Left One flue liner is false on this exterior chimney. As with all herringbone bond, the inset is at a 45° angle. Corbeling embellishes the chimney top for each flue.

Center, Right Protruding headers spiral around the upper part of this chimney. Stretchers protrude from the wider base, providing texture. Corbeled courses adorn the tops of the base and chimney and a cone-shaped crown makes the chimney appear taller.

Bottom, Right Larger brick were used for the herringbone bond on this chimney. The insets are surrounded by bullnose brick. The same bullnose stretchers also are used for the corbeled courses.

Fireplace Styles

When choosing a fireplace for your home, it is best to begin with a basic style that will fit into the designated area. After you have chosen the style, the fireplace can be personalized to incorporate the material and special features you desire. The drawings below are the typical fireplace styles found in homes today. Use this page as a guide when choosing your fireplace style.

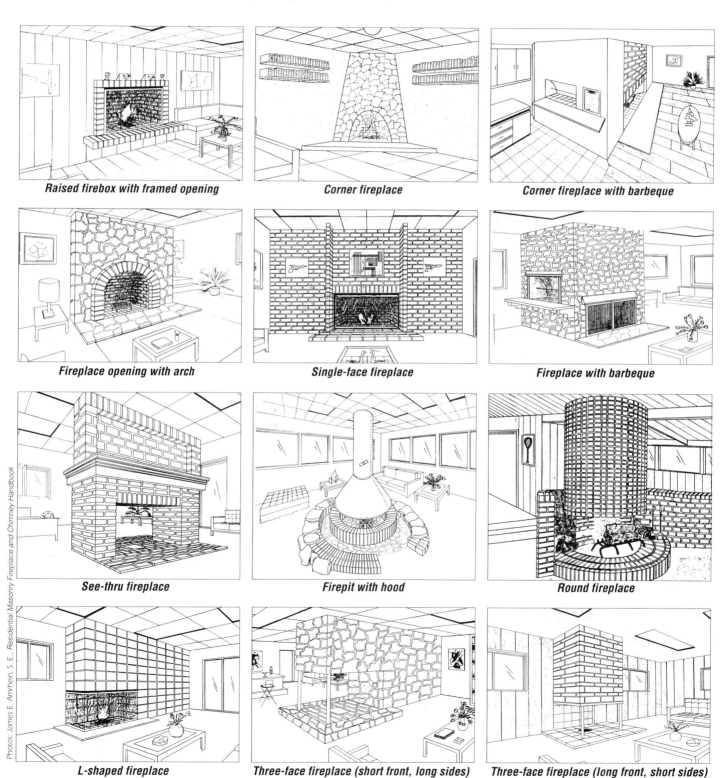

Raised firebox with framed opening

Corner fireplace

Corner fireplace with barbeque

Fireplace opening with arch

Single-face fireplace

Fireplace with barbeque

See-thru fireplace

Firepit with hood

Round fireplace

L-shaped fireplace

Three-face fireplace (short front, long sides)

Three-face fireplace (long front, short sides)

Photos: James E. Amrhein, S. E. *Residential Masonry Fireplace and Chimney Handbook*

The history of the Rumford fireplace

Count Rumford was an employee of the Bavarian government who lived in England in the late 1700s. In 1796 and 1798, he wrote two papers setting forth standards for the construction of an efficient fireplace. His goal was to design the fireplace so that radiant heat would be reflected back into the room.

In the Rumford design, the firebox is shallow with a high, wide opening. Its sides (covings) are widely flared from back to front. The firebox is constructed of white-washed brick or flat stones, rather than iron. All of these features help reflect heat. A more streamlined throat helps eliminate smoke without losing heated air up the chimney.

Rumford's fireplace was considered state-of-the-art until the 1850s, when wood-burning fireplaces temporarily went out of style. Thomas Jefferson had Rumford fireplaces built in Monticello and Thoreau even listed them among the modern conveniences that everyone took for granted. Though today's conventional fireplace generally is used mainly for atmosphere, the older Rumford design is still being built when efficient room heating is desired.

Information source: Jim Buckley, Buckley Rumford Fireplace Co., Columbus, OH, and the book *Residential Masonry Fireplace and Chimney Handbook* by James E. Amrhein, S.E.

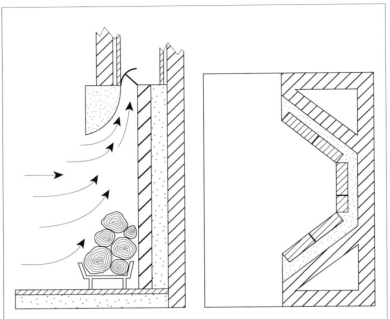

Rumford fireplace drawings were adapted from Rumford's 1795 Plates, Numbers 3 and 14. *Courtesy Jim Buckley.*

How to care for your fireplace

The National Fire Protection Association recommends that chimneys be inspected and if necessary, cleaned, at least once a year to ensure that they are clear, sound, free from combustible deposits, and have adequate draft.

Assessing a chimney flue's condition takes a practiced eye. It is important to use an experienced, Certified Chimney Sweep®. A Certified Chimney Sweep® is one who has passed extensive professional tests given by the National Chimney Sweep Guild.

In evaluating your fireplace's chimney, the sweep will check the flue for accumulation of soot and/or creosote on the flue walls, excessive moisture, proper draft, and any damage that may be considered hazardous. Sometimes a sweep will recommend videoscanning. A masonry chimney that isn't too far gone can be repaired, lined, and waterproofed.

® Registered certification mark of the National Chimney Sweep Guild.

Information source: Jay Hensley, editor/publisher, SNEWS, The Chimney Sweep News, an independent trade magazine for chimney sweep professionals. P.O. Box 98, Wilmore, KY 40390.

How to build a fire

The following suggestions will help you get more heat from your wood, reduce creosote deposits, and lessen air pollution.

Preparing Firewood
Firewood should be split and stacked under cover in the the early spring to be ready for burning in the fall. Dry firewood should be used, because it burns up to 25% more efficiently, produces fewer creosote deposits, ignites faster, smokes less, and is lighter to carry. Hardwoods and softwoods are chemically similar, but they differ in density. Hardwoods are denser, so they produce a longer-lasting fire.

Starting the Fire
When starting a fire use plenty of crumpled newspaper and kindling. At least ten pieces of kindling should be placed on top of a large amount of loosely crumpled newspaper. Softwoods make the best kindling. Loosely stacked wood (crisscrossed) will burn quickly; a more compact load will burn slower.

The fire should be positioned forward enough in the firebox so it will get plenty of air (without smoke coming into the room) and so the heat will radiate out into the room. A properly burning fire produces bright flames until the wood is reduced to charcoal—there should be no smoke visible in the fire.

Information source: John F. Gulland Associates Inc., Killaloe, Ontario. Gulland is a wood-heat consultant.

The anatomy of a masonry fireplace

An explanation of the major parts and what they do

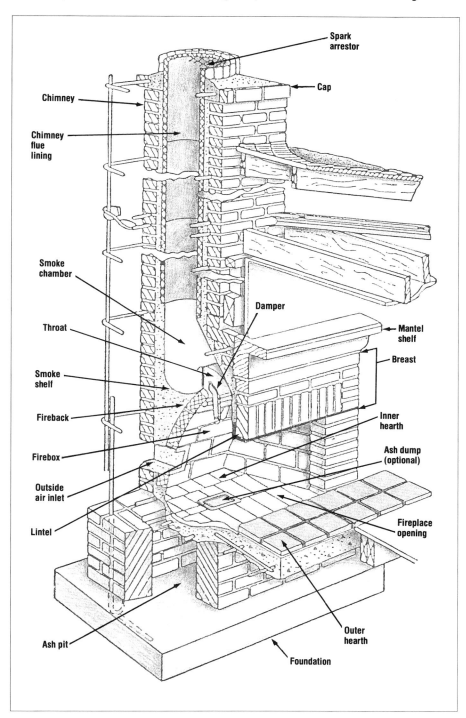

Spark arrestor

Cap

Chimney

Chimney flue lining

Smoke chamber

Damper

Mantel shelf

Breast

Throat

Smoke shelf

Fireback

Inner hearth

Ash dump (optional)

Firebox

Outside air inlet

Lintel

Fireplace opening

Ash pit

Outer hearth

Foundation

An explanation of parts follows:

Ash dump: Trap door to ash pit.

Ash pit: An optional, noncombustible storage compartment located below the firebox and used for dumping ashes. The ashes then don't have to be carried through the house.

Breast: Also called the fireplace face, the area above the fireplace opening and in front of the throat.

Cap: Should be sloped away from flue to prevent water from entering joint between flue and cap. Also improves the draft past the flue and flow of smoke exhaust. Caps that extend beyond the chimney face help keep water from running down the face. Flue liner should project about 2 inches above cap.

Chimney: The vertical structure that carries combustion gases to the outside. Height of chimney and size of flue determine the proper draft through the fireplace. For fire safety, top of chimney should be 3 feet above the highest point where the chimney penetrates the roof or 2 feet higher than any portion of the building within 10 feet of the chimney. It must be at least 2 inches from combustibles, or, if it's completely outside the structure, it must be 1 inch from combustibles. Walls of brick or concrete masonry chimneys should be at least 8 inches thick (unlined) or 4 inches thick (lined). Unlined walls of rubble stone chimneys should be at least 12 inches thick.

Damper: Used to regulate the draft from the firebox into the smoke chamber. Should extend the full width of the throat. Can be closed when fire isn't burning.

Fireback: The back wall of the firebox.

Firebox: The chamber where the fire is built. Usually constructed with firebrick laid with thin joints. Side walls are splayed outward to radiate heat into the room. The rear wall is sloped to provide an upward draft into the throat above. To allow for expansion and contraction, the 1-inch cavity between firebox walls and backup walls should be filled with noncombustible, compressible insulation, not mortar.

Fireplace opening: The opening through which the fire is built and viewed. The area of the fireplace opening determines the flue size that is required.

Flue lining: The channel inside the chimney that carries smoke and gases to the outside. Usually made of $\frac{5}{8}$-inch-thick clay liners that conform to ASTM C 315. Also can be made of pumice, cementitious materials, or metal. Should be laid up with nonwater-soluble calcium aluminate refractory cement mixture. Clay flue liners should be separated from chimney wall by an unfilled air space at least $\frac{1}{2}$ inch but not more than 1 inch wide. Liners begin at top of smoke chamber, where they should be supported by a ledge on at least three sides. Supporting masonry should not project past the inside of the flue. Flue liner should not slope more than 30° from vertical. Flue size depends on size of fireplace opening. Generally, the flue area must be $\frac{1}{10}$ the area of the fireplace opening, though some codes specify $\frac{1}{8}$ or $\frac{1}{12}$ under certain conditions. When more than one flue is contained in a chimney, a solid masonry wythe at least 4 inches thick should separate the flues. The separating wythe should be bonded to the chimney walls.

Footing: Should be concrete at least 12 inches thick and should extend at least 6 inches beyond the foundation walls on all sides.

Foundation walls: Made of masonry or cast-in-place concrete, usually unreinforced. Designed to support the weight of the chimney, resist frost action, and prevent settling or tipping of chimney. Most codes require foundation walls to be at least 8 inches thick.

Inner hearth: The floor of the fireplace. Usually made of fire-resistant brick.

Lintel: A steel angle or reinforced masonry beam located above the fireplace opening to support the face of the fireplace. Steel angle lintels should be at least $\frac{1}{4}$ inch thick, with a horizontal leg of at least $3\frac{1}{2}$ inches for use with nominal 4-inch brick or $2\frac{1}{2}$ inches for use with nominal 3-inch brick.

Mantel shelf: Decorative shelf above the fireplace opening that holds ornaments. Mantels that project more than $\frac{1}{8}$ inch for each inch away from the opening should be at least 12 inches from the opening.

Outer hearth: Made of brick, tile, or other noncombustibles. Supported by a structural slab or corbeled or cantilevered brick. Most codes require that it extend at least 8 inches on each side of the fireplace opening and 16 inches in front.

Outside air inlet: Reduces the amount of preheated room air used for combustion. For best performance, should be located in the sides or floor of the firebox, preferably in front of the grate. If it's located toward the back, ashes may be blown into the room. A stilling chamber constructed ahead of the inlet helps decrease the velocity of incoming air.

Smoke chamber: Funnels smoke and gases from the fire into the chimney flue. Should be symmetrically shaped so that the draft pulls evenly on the fire. The back wall is built vertical, but the side and front walls should be sloped (not more than 45°) toward the center to support the bottom of the flue lining. Walls should be parged to reduce friction and prevent smoke leakage. Smoke chamber height should not be greater than the inside width of the fireplace opening; its depth should not be greater than the depth of the firebox.

Smoke shelf: Prevents a downdraft from entering firebox and blowing smoke into the room. Also catches soot and thus keeps fireplace cleaner. May be curved or flat.

Spark arrester: A screen on top of the flue that prevents sparks and other burning material from blowing out the chimney. Made of corrosion-resistant wire mesh with openings not larger than $\frac{1}{2}$ square inch.

Throat: Slot directly above the firebox through which smoke and gases pass into smoke chamber. Should be fitted with a damper. Should not be less than 8 inches above the highest point of the fireplace opening.

This article is reprinted from the September 1989 issue of *Aberdeen's Magazine of Masonry Construction.*

Masonry Heaters meet today's needs

Efficient fuel use, low emissions, and even, comfortable heat
have sparked renewed interest in masonry stoves

By J. Patrick Manley

During Europe's "Little Ice Age," from the mid-1500s through the mid-1800s, temperatures were well below what is considered normal today. Wood was the primary fuel source, and as its consumption increased, shortages became widespread. Air quality, already a problem from inefficient open fireplaces, also was getting worse.

Masons who realized the heat retention value of stone, brick, and tile began to experiment with more efficient means of heating masonry mass with a wood fire. They discovered that wood could be burned efficiently and with little smoke by enclosing the fire within masonry, burning a hot fire, and passing the fire and exhaust gases through masonry baffles or channels.

Over the centuries, as masonry stove use increased, innumerable variations of material, shape, and flue design have been created.

Finns used native soapstone to fashion their heaters. Soapstone is beautiful and easily carved. It has remarkable heat-retention properties and the ability to withstand the thermal shock of a hot fire.

Sweden has a tradition of tall, round, or rectangular tile and stucco heaters, many of which are centuries old and still in use today.

In central Europe and Russia, masonry heaters were the heart of the home. Built of tile or brick, they were used to bake, cook, and smoke foods and to heat water. Heated benches and even sleeping platforms on top were common.

One wonders why more immigrants to the Americas from Europe didn't bring the idea with them. One theory holds that stove masons were highly regarded, well-established tradesmen who weren't interested in open land and farming. Besides, America was fully forested. Frugal use of fuel wasn't needed.

Interest in masonry heaters revived during the energy crisis of the mid-1970s. As people searched for efficient alternative fuel sources, some investigated the European tradition of masonry stoves and began to build them in North America. In the years following, they have passed on what they've learned through magazine articles, books, and dozens of hands-on workshops.

Heaters, not just fireplaces

The main difference between an open masonry fireplace and a masonry heater is the efficiency of the fire and the amount of pollution released. The firebox is smaller in a heater, because too large a firebox reduces combustion efficiency and causes unnecessary thermal stress.

Glass or metal doors with draft controls are necessary in a heater. The doors control the amount of air entering the firebox. Too much air cools the fire and too little air starves the fire. Both result in low combustion efficiency and increased pollutants. The hotter the fire, the higher the combustion efficiency and the lower the amount of pollutants produced. Masonry heaters routinely operate with firebox temperatures of 1,500° F to 2,000° F.

Another major difference is the path the exhaust follows from the firebox to the chimney. The open fireplace allows the exhaust to vent directly out the chimney. Little of the heat produced is radiated into the room, and the rest goes up the stack. The underutilized masonry mass doesn't absorb much heat. Once the fire is out, little retained heat is available to continue heating.

Upon leaving a masonry heater's firebox, hot gases flow through specially designed masonry channels or flues. Ten to thirty feet of flues distribute the heat throughout the mass and keep the exhaust gases within the heater longer, giving more time for heat transfer. The masonry mass absorbs 75% to 90% of the energy released from the burn.

Heaters and metal stoves

Masonry heaters and metal stoves have an abundance of striking differences: safety, size, weight, method of firing, emissions, and fuel economy.

The surface temperature of a metal stove is 400° F to 500° F, hot enough to burn skin before you know you're burned. The operating surface temperature of a masonry heater is 150° F to 250° F. Casual contact will not burn skin. The larger surface area radiates a constant, even heat, which is 60% radiant and 40% convective. Brick and other masonry materials transfer heat at a much lower rate than cast iron or steel.

A conventional metal stove controls fire by starving it of oxygen. The low combustion temperatures fail to ignite a large percentage of gases produced during the wood burning process. This shows up as smoke out of the chimney and creosote formed in the chimney.

In a masonry heater those gases, which require combustion temperatures of 1,100° F to ignite, are readily burned off. Creosote won't form because the gases that create it are burned.

Current EPA standards limit emissions from conventional wood stoves to 7.5 grams of particulate matter per hour. Tests performed at Virginia Polytechnic Institute on masonry heaters have shown average emissions of 1 to 2 grams per hour.

Sometimes a masonry heater is thought to take up more floor space than a metal stove. When the unusable space required as clearance around a metal stove is factored in, however, the difference in footprint is negligible.

A metal stove needs constant tending to keep a fire going 24 hours a day. A masonry heater only needs a fire for a few hours, once or twice a day. There need never be a fire burning overnight or when no one is home.

Any fireplace or wood stove works better with dry wood. This is equally important with a masonry heater. A maximum 20% moisture content is ideal. But for a masonry heater, you don't need a long-lasting bed of coals, so you can burn a greater variety of wood. Softwoods, not good for a metal stove because they burn too hot and fast, can be excellent fuel for a masonry heater.

After a fire has burned down, the damper in the flue should be closed to prevent stored heat from going up the stack until the next firing. All the stored heat then slowly radiates to heat the home for the next 12 to 24 hours.

A masonry heater will not provide instant heat as a metal stove can. There is a 1- to 4-hour time lag from initial firing to bring the masonry mass from stone cold up to operating temperature. The

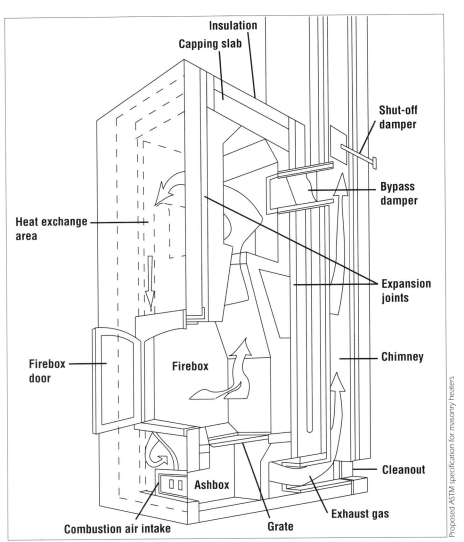

Cutaway view of a contraflow heater shows the path of heat and flue gases through the masonry mass.

time lag depends on the size of the heater and the masonry materials used. Once in daily operation, however, the heater never feels cool but rather radiates a constant, even heat.

Custom heaters

Ten years ago, virtually all heaters in North America were custom-designed and built with locally available materials. The advantage of such a heater is that it can be designed to suit the builder and the homeowner. A competent heater builder can use almost any locally available brick, fieldstone, or granite.

One popular design has the firebox located in the basement and the flue system within a masonry mass on the floor above. The masonry upstairs could have warming or baking ovens facing the kitchen or dining area. Another side could have hot seats or benches, or even an open fireplace.

Considerable precision is necessary in the construction of a quality custom heater, but it is not difficult for a competent mason to master. The work involves a fair amount of cutting and fitting firebrick. Cast refractory firebox and flue system kits are now available that save much time. After the core

Proposed ASTM specification for masonry heaters

is assembled, simply face it with any masonry material.

Because of the extreme heat, expansion joints are needed around the firebox and part of the flue system. Space must be maintained to prevent the hot core from expanding against the facing. A stove mason learning to build heaters must understand the coefficients of expansion of the various materials used in the heater. Refractory brick are used for the firebox and sometimes for the flue system. The firebox typically is no more than 18 inches wide. Its depth can vary from 12 to 30 inches. Height is determined by the style of the heater.

In Maine, the cost for an average custom brick stove to heat a 1,200-square-foot area is $5,000. This price includes heater materials and installation, but not the construction of the chimney or base. Prices will vary across the country based on locally available materials and labor costs.

One Austrian company offers a middle ground between custom-built and manufactured heaters. Their cores are individually designed to meet each client's needs. The homeowner then selects from among hundreds of possible combinations of type, style, and color. Prices range from $7,000 to $15,000 plus $900 to $2,000 for shipping and installation.

Manufactured models

In the past 10 years, a number of excellent manufactured masonry heaters have appeared. One company produces Finnish-designed soapstone heaters for the North American market. In this type of heater, often called a contraflow, flames rise to the top of the fireplace, then flow back down to the bottom through channels located on both sides of the firebox. Flue gases then exit at the bottom of the heater out the back.

These soapstone heaters range in size from 2,000 pounds (able to heat 650 square feet of living space) to 7,000 pounds (good for

1,500 square feet). Retail prices range from $3,000 to $9,000, plus $900 to $2,500 for shipping and installation. Excluding base preparation and chimney, installation takes 1 to 4 days.

One Swedish manufacturer makes an elegant masonry heater that follows a centuries-old design similar to the contraflow, but it has a longer flue run and a top exit. These stoves are rectangular or round and faced with stucco, porcelain tile, or soapstone. All are about 7½ feet tall with a 2x3-foot footprint. The Swedish stoves weigh between 3,500 and 4,000 pounds, heat 500 to 1,500 square feet, and cost $3,860 to $6,130, plus $1,000 to $2,000 shipping and installation.

Planning a masonry heater

Home size and layout determine heater size and placement. The larger the area to be heated, the more open a layout is preferred. Central location also is important. The more it is to be used as a primary heat source, the more central the heater should be. In Western Europe and Scandinavia, though, many homes have multiple heaters for different areas because the owners prefer to heat just the areas in use.

Though many architects are enthusiastic about masonry heaters and some promote them, most masonry heaters now are built for the homeowner who has learned the ways of heaters. Ideally, a stove builder should be contacted when a new home is in the design stage. That way, the heater can best be integrated aesthetically and functionally into the home. Details such as getting outside air to the heater also can be worked out more easily. This is important, because today's tight homes may not allow enough air in for proper combustion, especially when a kitchen or bathroom exhaust fan is in use.

On the other hand, installing a masonry stove in an existing home is no more difficult than retrofitting with a fireplace or metal stove and

chimney. In fact, because a masonry heater's low surface temperature generally allows less clearance to combustible surfaces, often it is easier to integrate one into an existing home. Required clearances are governed by local building codes, however, and will vary.

Becoming a stove mason

I've been a self-employed brick and stone mason for 20 years. After reading a newspaper article about heaters 12 years ago, I decided to specialize in masonry heaters. Little information was available in this country at that time, so I, like many other heater masons, made several trips to Europe to learn more about their design and construction. Now there is an abundance of information on masonry heaters. Besides dozens of magazine articles, there are also good books on the subject (Refs. 1 and 2).

The Masonry Heater Association of North America (MHA), established in 1986, combines the experience of dozens of the best heater builders. MHA has played a leading role in the development of emissions test methods for masonry heaters and has developed a draft standard through ASTM for masonry heater construction.

It feels good to bring masonry into another facet of daily life. Stone and brick are the oldest, most basic, and most beautiful building materials known. Add modern refractory materials, cast or fabricated doors and fittings, and you have a safe, efficient masonry heater of lasting beauty.

J. Patrick Manley is a mason and stove builder, the owner of The Brick Stove Works, Washington, ME.

References
1. David Lyle, The Book of Masonry Stoves, 1984, Brick House Publishing Co. Inc., Andover, MA.
2. Albert Barden, and Heikki Hyytiainen, The Heart of the Home, 1988, Building Books Ltd.

Reprinted from the September 1991 issue of Aberdeen"s Magazine of Masonry Construction.

Index